SIMON ELLIOTT

# THE ELLIOTT FAMILIES

## 1762-1911

### A HISTORY AND GENEALOGY WITH BIOGRAPHIES

SHOWING CONNECTIONS WITH THE TERWILLIGAR, HUMPHREY AND RAMSEY FAMILIES

*By*
SIMON ELLIOTT

PRINCETON, ILLINOIS
1911

# CONTENTS

---

## ILLUSTRATIONS

# PREFACE

Nearly everybody who writes the genealogy of a family finds, sooner or later, that the undertaking is greater and more difficult than was expected. I began this work, mainly through correspondence, six years ago, trying to locate somebody who had escaped "the pale horse and his rider" long enough to have learned something of the traditions that have come down to us from our ancestry. I have not been very successful in finding such persons, and am surprised to learn how little nearly all of us know about our own people.

To the many kind friends who have furnished valuable information with family records etc., I herewith acknowledge great indebtedness, and return sincere thanks to each and all.

Especially am I indebted to Mrs. Anna Martha Moss, (granddaughter of William Elliott, who was a brother of my grandfather, John Elliott, (1) and who was one of the only two survivors of the wreck of the Faithful Steward, in Mahogany Bay on the coast of New Jersey) of Paden, Oklahoma, for nearly all that I have learned about the descendants of her grandfather.

Horace H. Elliott of Chicago has also rendered much valuable assistance in gathering material for the work and in its publication. Mrs. Kate B. Maple and William S. Morrill also are deserving of mention in this connection, having furnished me pictures of the old house and the graves. And now, at the end of it all, there is a feeling of disappointment—that it is not as complete as I would like; but I have not purposely ignored anybody and have made an honest effort to get all the information obtainable under the circumstances.

After I got this work fairly started there was a space of three or four years in which there was little progress made with it, owing in a measure to my own physical infirmities; but my son, E. F. Elliott, recently returned home and has done much that was necessary to finish the work. Some sketches that he has written are followed by his initials.

I realize that the record of many branches of the family is very incomplete and will be a disappointment to them as well as myself, and I hope that some younger person may be encouraged to take this as a basis and publish a book that will be complete. There are perhaps not more than a half dozen people living who have heard, from the older descendants of John and William Elliott, the story of the shipwreck and it was mainly with a view of preserving this early history, by having it published, that I began the work. I did not expect then to make it complete as regards the later generations and even if I had, my age, and my desire to have it published in the near future, precludes, the possibility of doing so. That there will be errors in dates in this work there is little doubt. In fact dates that will appear correct to some will seem erroneous to others, as some of them are a matter of memory and not of record and in some instances members of the same family disagree.

The name (Elliott), so far as I know, is always spelled the same way by all the descendants of John and William Elliott; but others spell it in various ways. Gen. Isaac H. Elliott, now living at Dexter, N. M., sent me an article from the Los Angeles Times, written by a special contributor, concerning prominent men of the name who were conspicuous in the affairs of the world from the days of William the Conqueror down to comparatively recent times.

It is impossible, of course, for me to determine the relationship between the Elliotts mentioned in this article and those of our own branch of the family, but that a relationship does exist there is little doubt, and for that reason I have thought it proper to reprint the article in full.

It is, however, to be regretted that in numerous cases valuable statistics might have been added if continued requests had not been met with entire indifference, and were often void of recognition.

Once again expressing the hope that this partial and necessarily imperfect work may stimulate some future historian to more complete efforts, I present it to its readers, sincerely trusting that it may be of some little value to those descendants of our common ancestry.

Simon Elliott

Princeton, Ill. A. D. 1911.

# THE ELIOT FAMILY

THE FIRST BOOK PRINTED IN THIS COUNTRY
WORK OF AN ELIOT

*By Eleanor Lexington*

Eliot, by some authorities, is said to be derived from the old Hebrew name Elias, which means Jehovah, or Yahver, is my God. The literal translation of the root

ELIOT

Eli is "elevation," or, more freely rendered, judge, high priest. Other derivatives are Eliah, my God is father; Elieger, God is help, and Elihu, God is He.

Variations of the name Eliot besides the more common forms Eliott, Elliot and Elliott, are Ellis, Ellison, Elson, Elliotson, Eliett, Ellet, Elley, Ellery, Eleot, Elyot, Ellyeta, Elyotte, Eyllyott, Lelliot and Aliot. The Norman knight, William de Aliot, was the first who began to make history; from his time on to the end of the fourteenth century the name began with "A;" it was then replaced by "E."

When William the Conqueror first set foot upon English soil he stumbled and fell, but he had the presence of mind to turn the omen to advantage by crying out that he had taken possession of the country, and a soldier running to a cottage took some thatch, which he presented to his general, as if giving him seigin of the kingdom. Just here comes an Eliot upon the scene. Sir William de Aliot drew his sword and swore by the honor of a soldier that he would maintain, at the hazard of his blood, the right of his lord to the sovereignty of the country. For this right worthy and loyal bearing, William added to his coat of arms the motto Per Saxa, Per Ignes, Fortiter et Recte.

Skipping over a few centuries and past others of the family who have been bright and shining lights in their several ways and generation, we come to another doughty warrior, George Augustus Eliott, always and forever known as the defender of Gibraltar. He had distinguished himself during the seven years war in Germany, but it was Gibraltar which gave him the opportunity of his life; there he withstood a siege perhaps unparalleled in the history of civilized warfare. He was honored with the title Lord Heathfield, Baron of Gibraltar, and an addition granted to his arms—the castle of Gibraltar for crest and the legend of Plus Ultra. His shield was the same as that reproduced with this sketch. The title became extinct with his son.

The Eliot family can point to its martyr, Sir John Eliot, pure patriot and eloquent statesman, who paid the price of consistency to principle with his head. This in the troublous times of Charles I. The prime pilot of his time was Hugh Elyot, who with one other discovered Newfoundland in 1527. He was from Somersetshire, where descendants of de Aliot settled; Devon and Cornwall were also their strongholds, particularly Port Eliot, Cornwall. There is also a town in the north of Scotland called Eliot. One of the Lord Eliots of Port Eliot was an early patron of Joshua Reynolds. Nearer our own time, we find that Queen Victoria's valued adviser, especially on family matters, was Edward Eliot, the third Earl of St. Germans.

When the ship Lyon dropped anchor in Plymouth Harbor, about ten years after the arrival of the Mayflower, the first Eliot arrived. He was John Eliot, Apostle to the Indians. The first entry on the record of "marriages" of Roxbury, Mass., was that of Eliot and Hanna Mumford, September 1, 1632. To use his own words, she proved "a dear, faithful, pious, prudent, prayerful wife."

Of their six children, the only one who left descendants of the Eliot name was Rev. Joseph Eliot of Guilford, Ct. Fitz Greene Halleck and Prof. Elisha Mitchell were of this branch of the Eliot family.

In Salem, one of the jurors of the witchcraft trials was Andrew Eliot, who came to this country in 1670. For the part he took in helping to condemn witches, so called, to death, he afterward reproached himself bitterly, declaring that he would do "none of such things again on such grounds for the whole world."

In King Philip's War we find Henry Eliot took part. John and David Eliot were brothers, and from New Hampshire were early on the ground at the battle of

Bunker Hill, and in the hottest of the fight. Each man had but a gill of powder and fifteen balls dealt out to him. David Eliot had only his fowling piece, which after a few rapid discharges became dangerous to handle. Just then he discovered a good musket on the ground, which he quickly appropriated. David was a surveyor, and surveyed nearly half of the State of New Hampshire, James Eliot of Massachusetts was in the Revolution, also Andrew Eliot, who was but a youth at the outbreak of hostilities. Maj. Bernard Elliott commanded at Fort Moultrie in the War of Independence, and its first flag was made by his wife. "Stand by these colors," she said, "so long as they wave in the air of liberty."

At the meetings of the Eliot Family Association many interesting anecdotes are told and traditions passed along. The first reuinon of the descendants of John Eliot, Apostle, was held at Guilford, Ct., in 1875. Other meetings have been held under an old oak, the meeting-house, as it was called, of the Apostle, at South Natick, Mass. Relics brought together at such times are an Indian Bible and a Bay psalm book; the latter was the first book printed in this country, in Cambridge, Mass., 1640. Copies are so rare that one has been sold for $1200. Of Eliot's Indian Primer but two copies are extant, of which one is in the British Museum.

It has been suggested that John Eliot's wife was the first Christian Scientist. Her husbands' gifts to charity and his small salary made it difficult for her to obtain subsistence for her family. She perhaps nourished them upon the solid pabulum of mental suggestion.

One of the number at a recent family reunion dropped into poetry anent the orthography of the name:

"They have doubled the 'l'
To make it swell;
They have added the 't'
To be odd, you see.
Some have put a 'y'
In the place of an 'i,'
But still it spells
E-l-i-o-t."

One reason thus did the great Eliot spell his name. The coat of arms reproduced is azure in bend, a baton or crest, a hand coupled at the wrist in armor, holding a cutlass in bend. Motto, Per Saxa, Per Ignes, Fortiter et Recte—over rocks, through fire, bravely and honorably. Of the colors emblazoned, or denotes generosity and elevation of mind, azure loyalty and truth. An arm is armor, one fitted for the performance of his enterprises; a sword, justice and military honor, or virtue in warlike deeds.

Modifications of these arms were borne by most of the Scottish and some of the English branches of the family. In the sixteenth century the Devonshire and Cornwall families adopted arms, argent, a fess gules between four cotises wavy azure; a mullet for difference. Crest, an elephant's head. This is found in the Visitation of Devonshire, 1620. One Eliot arms in the Visitation of Cornwall has twelve quarterings. Eliot arms are quartered with the Mintos of Scotland and with the Suffolks. If such matters were of value it would be easy to trace the Eliots through various families back to royalty itself. Perhaps on this account the motto Precedentibus Instar—in the footsteps of your ancestors —was adopted. Other Eliot mottoes are Occurent Nubes, clouds will intervene, and Non Sine Deo, not without God.

# ELLIOTT FAMILY GENEALOGY

In gathering material for this brief sketch of the genealogy of the Elliott families the writer has failed to learn, from any reliable source, that there is any record in this country extending farther back than the sailing of the Faithful Steward, on which vessel the family sailed for America from Londonderry, Ireland, about, and probably in the year 1785, and it has been necessary to rely for information on the dim traditions which have filtered down through the generations to the surviving descendants of John and William Elliott.

About the year 1784 John Elliott, the oldest son, then about 22 years of age, was sent by his father to America on the vessel Lazy Mary, to see what the country was like and with instructions that if at the end of a year he thought they had better move there, he was to write them to do some impossible thing.

They were wealthy people, had a large house, and at the appointed time he wrote them that he had been unable to build himself a house and asked them to send theirs over to him. Knowing what that meant, they at once prepared to move. This precaution was probably considered necessary because of the fact that all young men owed a certain number of years of military service to the government, and should he have written them to come and his letter have fallen into the hands of the authorities, they would probably not have been allowed to leave the country until such military service had been performed.

When they sailed the party consisted of the father, five daughters, and two sons, Simon and William. There were also a number of cousins named Stewart and Lee, among them Mary Lee, a young lady of most remarkable grace and beauty. During the voyage the captain of the vessel became wildly infatuated with her and when they were nearing the American shore he told her of his affection for her. But she refused to consider his proposal or listen to his plea. This so mortified and disheartened him that he said he did not care what became of himself or his vessel, and in his despondency he got helplessly drunk. They were sailing along the coast of New Jersey in Mahogany Bay, on whose rocky shores many good ships have ended their last voyage. A gathering storm soon struck the ship, practically helpless without the guiding hand of the captain, and drove it on the rocks where the furious waves of the bay soon pounded it to pieces. All on board were drowned except the two brothers, Simon and William, who undertook to swim ashore and were thrown up on the beach in an unconscious condition, but finally survived. When the ship began to go to pieces, and all on board, except the drunken captain, realized that their last hour had come, the father brought out two bags of gold and asked his sons if they thought they could reach the shore with it. They looked at the gold which probably represented a considerable portion of their wealth, then at the storm that was sweeping everything to destruction, the huge breakers that were thundering against the rocks, and told him that if they could get ashore with their lives it was all they could hope for and that there was little hope even of that.

There is a tradition that there was a third brother on the ship, a little boy named Andrew, and that one of his brothers, Simon or William, tried to swim ashore with him on his back, but Mrs. Anna Martha Moss, of Paden, Oklahoma, who is the only living granddaughter of William Elliott, and to whom I am indebted for much valuable information in connection with this work, writes me that she never heard of any such boy and that she is positive there were but two brothers aboard the vessel. The two survivors of the wreck fell into the hands of wreckers or land pirates who infested the New Jersey Coast at that time. Many chests and boxes containing valuable goods belonging to the family were washed ashore and recognized by the two brothers, but everything was taken by those bandits of the coast, the owners not daring to claim anything and being glad to escape with their lives. These two brothers, stranded on a desolate shore in a strange country without money or friends and but scant clothing, finally made their way to Pennsylvania where they found their brother John. The scenes among the passengers during the wrecking of the vessel were so frightful, so full of terror and despair, that no tongue or pen could describe them, and these men even after they had grown old could rarely be induced to talk about it.

Away back somewhere in the dim past someone wrote a song of many verses concerning the Elliotts, Lees, and Stewarts, the shipwreck and the marvelous beauty of Mary Lee. Old people, who used to read less and sing more than we do now, sang this song and it was very popular and sensational with them seventy-five or one hundrd years ago. As a literary effort it could hardly be considered a success but it tells something of the tragic tale that has come down to us in song and story through the intervening years. So far as I know there is no one who remembers any of this song except Mrs. Moss (previously mentioned), who sent me the following verses written from memory;

The Elliotts and the Lees
  And Stewarts of great fame,
They may lament and mourn
  For the lands they've left behind.

They may lament and mourn
  As long as they have days,
For their friends and relations
  Lie in Mahogany's bays.

As for that lovely damsel
  Called Mary Lee by name,
Her beauty in particular
  I mean for to proclaim.

Many handsome young men
  On her did cast their eyes,
But to our great misfortune
  Among the dead she lies.

Simon Elliott, who was a survivor of the wreck of the Faithful Steward, after living several years in Pennsylvania and Virginia, came west and located at the mouth of Copperas Creek, in Fulton County, Illinois, about five miles from Canton. The country was then new, land was cheap, and the rate of interest on money was high. He bought land at government prices, loaned money and became wealthy. He had no family, lived and died a bachelor, and his estate which was settled by his nephew, John Elliott (2), was divided among the children of his brothers, William and John, sixteen of them in all. I have failed to learn the date of his birth or exact date of his death, which occurred in either 1843 or 1844.

William Elliott, the other survivor of the wreck of the Faithful Steward, married Sarah Wilke, or Wilkey,

*Photographed, February, 1911.*

THE HOMESTEAD OF JOHN ELLIOTT (1)

LOCATED NEAR REMINGTON, HAMILTON COUNTY, OHIO

It was here that he grew from boyhood to manhood, and his children were all born in this house. The walls of the house are of stone, two feet in thickness, and were built about the year 1800.

in Pennsylvania. They had eleven children named Charles, Andrew, John, Simon, Elizabeth, Isabel, James, Mary Jane and Sarah Ann who were twins, William and Elinore. None of them are living now, with the exception of Charles, who died young, all of them lived to be old. They all moved to Muskingum County, Ohio and later to near Birmingham and Fairfield, Iowa, except Andrew and James who remained in Ohio. Some of Andrew's grandchildren are living there yet, but James had no children.

John Elliott (1) was born of protestant parents in northern Ireland in 1762. That part of Ireland was originally settled by protestant Scotch people, and it is probable that the Elliotts, Lees and Stewarts, were descendants of those old Scotch families. He came to this country, about 1784, a year or two previous to the sailing of the rest of the family. He was married in Pennsylvania about 1786 to Mary Miller, who was born July 15th, 1767, and died near Remington, Hamilton County, Ohio, September 26th, 1840, aged 73 years. She was of German descent and was the sister of Sarah Lackey, who lived and died near Montgomery, Ohio, and Nancy Stewart, who has many descendants in Bureau and Marshall Counties, Illinois, as well as in Ohio.

After their marriage they settled (probably in the spring of 1787), on a millsite that he had previously discovered on the Little Miami river at the mouth of Sycamore creek, in Hamilton County, Ohio, fourteen miles from where Cincinnati now is. For some time after their arrival there and until they built for themselves a cabin, they lived in an immense sycamore tree, whose interior had decayed until it formed a room eleven feet in diameter. At first thought it might seem that they had rather limited room, but their quarters were doubtless both more spacious and more comfortable than many have who are settling on the western prairies today. It was from this great tree that Sycamore creek derived its name. When they moved, their personal effects consisted of a horse, a cow, a gun, an axe, and some small articles that the bride carried on the horse which she rode. The dense growth of heavy timber along the river and over the surrounding country was full of thievish and hostile Indians who annoyed them greatly for several years. Once having heard that they were in danger of being massacred they took the horse and cow and a few things they could gather up hurriedly and carry conveniently and went down the Miami river to Fort Columbia, now Columbia. That night the Indians massacred the white people at Bloody Run. This was of course only one of the many disadvantages under which they labored but they had sagacity, energy, courage, health and physical ability, and these are the characteristics that win in any country. They paid for, cleared, fenced, and farmed their land, planted an orchard, raised and educated a family of six children, three sons and three daughters, and later when the children were grown built a dam across the river, a flour mill, a saw mill, a wool carding mill, and a distillery. They sent the products of the mill and distillery, together with the pork which they packed, down the Ohio and Mississippi rivers to New Orleans, where they were sold. They also built a very large two-story stone house where their daughters were married and their sons came home with their brides before going out into the world to fight life's battles for themselves. That big old stone house, whose walls are two feet thick, will probably be standing there when the names of its builders and their nearer descendants shall have perished from the memory of man. He died

March 20th, 1843, in the eighty-second year of his age, and was buried at Remington, Ohio, by the side of her, who was the mother of his children, and who for more than half a century had shared with him his joys and sorrows, his hopes and fears, and endured with him the hardships and privations incident to pioneer life. The names of their children were Simon, Elcy, Sarah, Isabel, William, and John, their birth being in the order named. I am told by Mrs. Hettie Johnston, whose mother was a daughter of Elcy Elliott, that there were three other children who died in infancy, two being buried at Columbia and one at Sycamore church near the old homestead. Mrs. Johnston got this information from her mother, and while it is doubtless correct, I never heard of it from any other source.

## SECOND GENERATION

### Family of Simon Elliott (2)

Simon Elliott (2), farmer and miller, b. April 4, 1788, near Remington, Ohio; m. Feb. 12, 1818, Maria Stinson, daughter of Samuel and Margaret Robinson, b. Jan. 9, 1799; d. April 4, 1881. He enlisted as a private in the army Aug. 11, 1812, was honorably discharged Feb. 15, 1813, and was Captain in the Ohio State Militia after the war. He died near Remington, Ohio, Mar. 18, 1853, but his wife died at Princeton, Ill., at the home of her son Simon, where she lived during her later years. Both are buried at Miamiville, Ohio. He was a free mason and a democrat, and while he had no desire for political life he had an extensive acquaintance with, and was popular among, the prominent men of his time. They had six children: Margaret Robinson (3), John (3), Samuel Robinson (3), Simon (3), Arthur (3), and James Finley (3).

## Third Generation and Descendants

Margaret R. Elliott (3), b. Aug. 2, 1820, near Remington, Ohio; d. Oct. 13, 1895, near Lincoln, Neb.; buried in Buckingham cemetery near the home; m. first, Oct. .., 1838, Benjamin Buckingham, farmer, b. Mar. 1, 1811, d. Sept. 30, 1851; m. second, June 25, 1854, Martin Hoover, farmer, b. June 15, 1807; d. July 12, 1886.

Children (Buckingham):
Maria (4) b. Aug. 31, 1842; d. May 8, 1853.
William (4) b. Aug. 23, 1845; d. May 12, 1853.
Harriet (4) b. June 28, 1847; d. Aug. 10, 1848.
Martha Ann (4) b. Nov. 3, 1849; d. May 13, 1853.

Children (Hoover): Risa Emeline (4), Martin (4), Abbie Day (4), and Arthur (4).
Risa E. Hoover (4) b. April 8, 1855 near Lacon, Ill., m. Nov. 25, 1874, John J. Strawn, retired business man, b. March 16, 1852.

Children (Strawn):
Infant son b. Dec. 1, 1879; d. Dec. 3, 1879.
John Elliott (5) b. Feb. 26, 1882; m. Sept. 30, 1906.
Lillian Estella Carlson b. Sept. 22, 1888.
Martin Hoover (4) farmer, b. Dec. 6, 1857 near Lacon, Ill.; m. Oct. 15, 1879 Elizabeth Remley b. Feb. 26, 1859.

Children (Hoover):
Lyle Remley (5) b. Dec. 20, 1898.
Lucille Maurine (5) b. Jan. 10, 1902.
Abbie D Hoover (4) b. March 16, 1861 near Lacon Ill.; m. Sept. 30, 1889 John W. Dougherty, machinist, b. Nov. 20, 1857.

Children (Dougherty):

Margaret Hoover (5) b. Aug. 25, 1893; d. Feb. 26, 1896.

Risa Bell (5) b. Sept. 1, 1897; d. Nov. 1, 1903.

Arthur Hoover (4), farmer, b. Nov. 12, 1862 near Lacon, Ill.; m. Sept, 11, 1889 Mae C. Ford b. July 24, 1866.

Children (Hoover):

Gene Ford (5) b. July 21, 1890; d. Nov. 8, 1908.

Helen Arthur (5) b. Sept. 6, 1891.

John Elliott (3) farmer, b. Dec. 6, 1821 near Remington, Ohio; d. Dec. 13, 1896 at Camp Dennison, Ohio; buried at Miamiville, Ohio; m. — — — 1848 Susanna Dawson, b. Sept. 14, 1825; d. Oct. 9, 1886; buried at Miamiville, Ohio.

Children (Elliott): Maria Melissa (4), Arthur (4), Mary Vest (4) James Servetus (4), and Laura Bell (4).

Maria M. Elliott (4) b. Jan. 31, 1849 near Remington, Ohio; single.

Arthur Elliott (4), railway employe, b. June 27, 1850, near Remington, Ohio; m. May 11, 1881, Adaline Jenifer, b. May 10, 1865.

Children (Elliott): Arthur Jenifer (5) b. Jan 24, 1882; m. — — Katherine S. Miller, b. Nov. 26, 1880; William Brunell (5) b. July. 15, 1885. d. Oct. 3, 1886.

Mary V. Elliott (4) b. Nov. 28, 1851 near Remington, Ohio; d. April 2, 1893; single.

James S. Elliott (4) farmer, b. Feb. 3, 1854 near Remington, Ohio; single.

Laura B. Elliott (4) b. Dec. 4, 1864 near Remington, Ohio; single.

Samuel R. Elliott (3) farmer, b. Sept. 1, 1824 near Remington, Ohio; d. June 10, 1899 at Montgomery, Ohio; buried at North Prairie Baptist Cemetery near Princeton, Ill.; came to Illinois early in 1854 and settled near Heaton's Point, six miles north-west of Princeton; lived there and in Princeton until the death of his first wife; after his second marriage lived at Montgomery, Ohio; m. first Dec. 18, 1854 Elizabeth Heaton, b. June 1, 1828; d. Apr. 28, 1888; buried at the North Prairie Baptist Cemetery; daughter of Reese Heaton, who came to Illinois at an early date from Trumbull County, Ohio; m. second, April 15, 1890 Castilla (Thompson) Stewart, b. March 19 1827; d. Sept. 24, 1909.

Children (Elliott): Alice Marion (4), Albert Heaton (4) and Ada Florence (4), all born near Princeton, Ill.

Alice M. Elliott (4) b. Oct. 11, 1855; m. first, June 1, 1879, James McKee Parks, b. Feb. 4, 1853, d. Sept. 21, 1883; m. second, Aug. 13, 1891 Frank D. Bryan, farmer, b. Nov. 2, 1860, whose first wife was her sister.

Children (Parks):

Daisey (5) b. April 4, 1881; d. May 17, 1881.

Albert H. Elliott (4), farmer, b. Oct. 30, 1860; m. Dec. 25, 1883, Maud D. Soash, b. April 20, 1867; d. Jan. 16, 1890.

Children (Elliott): Maud Alice (5) and Zelah Lucile (5).

Maud A. Elliott (5), b. Dec. 5, 1884; m. Sept. 27, 1910, George Schafer, farmer, b. Nov. 3, 1878.

Zela L. Elliott (5), b. Feb. 27, 1887; m. Sept. 25, 1910, Lee H. Huffstodt, farmer, b. July 10, 1885.

Ada F. Elliott (4) b. Nov. 1, 1863; d. Sept. 5, 1890; m. Jan. 27, 1885, Frank D. Bryan, farmer, b. Nov. 2, 1860.

Children (Bryan): Marion Elizabeth (5).

Marion E. Bryan (5), b. May 14, 1886; m. Jan. 25, 1906, Calvin Hoover, farmer, b. Dec. 15, 1882, near Princeton, Ill.

Children (Hoover):

Frank Ivan (6) b. April 21, 1907.

Merle Lee (6) b. Sept. 29, 1910.

Hon. Simon Elliott (3), a retired farmer living in Princeton, Ill., was born near Remington, Ohio, Feb. 10, 1827, and is now the oldest living descendant of John Elliott (1). He was educated in the common schools, and at Parker's Academy, Clermont County, Ohio; left Ohio Aug. 30, 1848, in company with Matthew G. Humphrey, and drove through to Princeton where they arrived Sept. 15, and the following year located on section seven, Dover Township, Bureau County, securing 160 acres of government land, for which he paid 75 cents an acre. He still owns this farm and it has the unique history of being the only one in the county which has been neither mortgaged nor transferred since the title passed from the government. He has always taken an active interest in political matters and public affairs, was several times supervisor of Dover Township and was one of the commissioners who supervised the building of the Court House in 1860. On Dec. 1, 1875, he moved into Princeton for the purpose of educating his children. He was elected member of the Legislature on the Greenback Labor ticket in Nov., 1878, serving one term; was elected vice-president of the Illinois State Board of

Agriculture in 1886 and again in 1888, serving four years. The fight of his life came up in the Illinois House of Representatives during the consideration of the Stock Yards bill which he had introduced. This bill proposed to control the stock yards charges by law, and was opposed by the stock yards company, nearly all the Chicago members, the Speaker of the House and the influence of all the railroads running into Chicago and East St. Louis. The member from the stock yards district, the Hon. Sol. Hopkins, was a man of good ability, a forcible debater, relentless in his opposition, unscrupulous in his methods, and prided himself on his superior knowledge of parliamentary law, by which he has succeeded in defeating all former attempts at control at previous sessions, few if any previous bills having reached the stage of second reading. He intimated that he would make short work of defeating the bill, and that "the old farmer" would be an easy victim. But in this case he was defeated in every attempt to "kill the bill" and it was ordered to second reading. It was regarded as the most important bill of the session, and several days later when it came up for discussion on its merits, the fighting was fast and furious for half a day between its friends and opponents, who fought over every inch of the ground with a desperation that surprised themselves as well as their friends. Hopkins and his friends were again defeated and the bill was ordered to third reading. After the battle of the day was over the older members of the house gathered around "the old farmer" and congratulated him on being the only man who had ever defeated Sol. Hopkins on parliamentary law, or fought him successfully on the floor of the house; but before the bill came up on third reading the secret influences that control so much of the legislation of the country had gotten in their work, and the bill failed to pass. The newspapers claimed, however, that it cost $50,000 to defeat it. (E. F. E.)

He was married April 23, 1856 at Low Point, Woodford County, Ill., to Sarah A. McCoy, third daughter of William and Jane McCoy, who was born in Brown County, Ohio, Jan. 28, 1833, and died in Princeton, Ill., Jan. 12, 1907. She was buried beside her two children who had preceded her to that far away country, of which we have heard so much, and know so little. For more than half a century, she shared with me the joys and sorrows, the successes and defeats, that are incident to human life. She took more than her share of the toils and privations of our earlier years.

The years rolled on, and "the pale horse and his rider" invaded our home, and took away the best friend I had on earth. The "grim monster" laid his icy hand on her loving heart and it ceased to beat. Her life blood froze in her veins, and she wilted like a flower cut down in a mid-summer day.

I find myself vainly asking, "Is there no redress, no appeal? Is this the final decree of the court of last resort? Won't she come back some day, like one returning from a pleasant journey?"

But the answer comes back with the echo, saying "Nevermore, nevermore."

Children: Edwin Forrest (4), Alfred Sumner (4), Kate (4), Nora (4), Lillian Bell (4) and Minnie Myrtle (4), all born near Princeton, Ill.

Edwin F. Elliott (4), railway employe, b. May 30, 1858; m. March 5, 1910.

Mary (Tobin) Seiler b. March 11, 1862.

Alfred S. Elliott (4), b. Dec. 28, 1860; d. May 24, 1868.

Kate Elliott (4), b. May 17, 1863; m. Sept 15, 1886.

Harry A. Gibbs, hardware merchant, b. Aug. 31, 1861.

Children (Gibbs):
Fred Elliott (5), Kathryn (5) and Winsor McCoy (5).
Fred E. Gibbs (5) b. July 26, 1887.
Kathryn Gibbs (5) b. June 26, 1894.
Winsor M. Gibbs (5) b. March 23, 1900.
Nora Elliott (4) b. March 3, 1866; d. Dec. 30th, 1867.
Lillian B. Elliott (4) b. Sept. 6, 1869; m. Aug. 11, 1894.
Burke Y. Benson, hotel man, b. May 6, 1869; d. Oct. 31, 1899.

Children (Benson):
Edwin Elliott (5) and Ada Lillian (5).
Edwin E. Benson (5) b. June 28, 1895.
Ada L. Benson (5) b. Jan. 2, 1897.
Minnie M. Elliott (4) b. Feb. 10, 1873; m. Feb. 18, 1907.
Charles A. Ashbaugh, civil engineer, b. Aug. 15, 1880.

Children (Ashbaugh):
John Elliott (5) and Anne Elliott (5).
John E. Ashbaugh (5) b. Sept. 24, 1908.
Anne E. Ashbaugh (5) b. Dec. 4, 1910.
Arthur Elliott (3), carpenter, b. March 20, 1830, near Remington, Ohio; d. Nov. 17, 1862 at Yellow Springs, Ohio and was buried there; m. Oct. 28, 1852, Achsah
Hayford b. June 6, 1829; d. Aug 9, 1874.

Children: Lizzie Robinson (4), Mary Hayford (4) and Myra Doane (4) (twins), Jessie (4) and Horace Hayford (4) (twins), all born at Yellow Springs, Ohio.

Lizzie R. Elliott (4) b. Aug. 10, 1853; d. Oct. 6, 1872. Single.
Mary H. Elliott (4) b. July 15, 1856; d. June 12, 1910; m. Dec. 7, 1873, Colin S. Avey, b. Dec. 29, 1857.

Children (Avey):

Arthur Elliott (5), Lottie Olive (5), Horace Milton (5), John Fountain (5), Jessie French (5), Cyrus Hayford (5) Edward Everett (5), Mary Alice (5), Ralph Grant (5) and William Colon (5).

Arthur E. Avey (5) b. Sept. 19, 1874; d. Nov. 3, 1902. Single.

Lottie O. Avey (5) b. April 23, 1877; m. Dec. 19, 1906, Wilford B. Ezell, b. July 30, 1872.

Children (Ezell):

Mary Eliza (6) b. Dec. 7, 1907. Jessie Frances (6) b. Mar. 4, 1911.

Horace M. Avey (5) b. July 13, 1880.

John F. Avey (5) b. May 18, 1884; m. Aug. 27, 1905 Ella A. Carter, b. Sept. 8, 1889.

Children: Lillian Beatrice (6) and Ella Lucile (6).

Lillian B. Avey (6) b. April 1, 1907.

Ella L. Avey (6) b. Sept 3, 1909.

Jessie F. Avey (5) b. March 28, 1887; m. Feb. 16, 1909, Thomas Lee Enderle, b. Sept. 27, 1880.

Child (Enderle):

Thomas Lee, b. Sept. 8, 1910.

Cyrus H. Avey (5) b. Jan. 2, 1890.

Edward E. Avey (5) b. July 11, 1892.

Mary A. Avey (5) b. Feb. 20, 1895.

Ralph G. Avey (5) b. Sept. 15, 1898.

William C. Avey (5) b. Sept. 6, 1901.

Myra D. Elliott (4) b. July 15, 1856; d. Oct. 14, 1890; m. March 28, 1888 William D. Beckett, b. Feb. 3, 1856.

Child (Beckett):

Arthur Elliott (5) b. Dec. 29, 1888.

Jessie Elliott (4) b. May 14, 1861; m. Aug. 8, 1888, William S. Morrill, b. Aug. 26, 1847.

Children (Morrill):

Horace Elliott (5), Charles Barnard (5), Mary Hayford (5), Elliott Wynn (5).

Horace E. Morrill (5) b. May 10, 1889.

Charles B. Morrill (5) b. Aug. 17, 1890; d. Oct. 2, 1902.

Mary H. Morrill (5) b. Aug. 21, 1892.

Elliott W. Morrill (5) b. Oct. 8, 1895.

Horace H. Elliott (4) Supt. Bureau Police Records Chicago, Ill., b. May 14, 1861; m. May 23, 1889 Annie Estella Conners, b. Sept. 3, 1861.

Child: Horace Arthur (5).

Horace A. Elliott (5) b. May 9, 1890; m. April 27, 1910, Elsie R. Venus, b. July 27, 1889.

Child: Mildred Ruth (6) b. June 8, 1911.

James F. Elliott (3), farmer, b. March 16, 1838, near Remington, Ohio; d. Feb. 16, 1909 at Manson, Iowa and is buried there; m. March 27, 1859, Laura Riker, b. July 31, 1840.

Children: Lillie Bell (4), Maggie May (4), Lyman Pingree (4), Simon Clinton (4) and Eva Lena (4).

Lillie B. Elliott (4) b. May 8, 1861. Single. Manager Gen. Mdse. Store.

Maggie M. Elliott (4) b. May 7, 1864; m. Jan. 2, 1887 Amos M. Bryan, farmer and stock breeder, b. Feb. 19, 1858.

Children (Bryan):

Zathoe (5) and Vivian (5).

Zathoe Bryan (5) b. Sept. 6, 1889.

Vivian Bryan (5) b. Feb. 6, 1891.

Lyman P. Elliott (4) civil engineer, b. Oct. 27, 1867; m. Feb. 26, 1906, Blanche A. Pond b. Oct. 21, 1876.

Simon C. Elliott (4) b. Oct. 5, 1871; d. in infancy.

Eva L. Elliott (4) b. May 5, 1877. Teacher. Single.

THE GRAVES OF JOHN ELLIOTT (I) AND MARY MILLER ELLIOTT, HIS WIFE

LOCATED NEAR REMINGTON, HAMILTON COUNTY, OHIO

## SECOND GENERATION

### Family of Elcy Elliott (2)

Elcy Elliott (2) b. Feb. 10, 1791, near Remington. Ohio; d. Nov. 19, 1858 near Montgomery, Ohio; m, March —, 1812, Nathaniel Terwilligar, farmer and mill-wright, b. May —, 1785; d. Sept. 4, 1835.

Children (Terwilligar):

John Elliott (3), Catherine Crist (3), Moses Kitchell (3), Mary Ann (3), Sarah Lackey (3), Eliza Crist (3), Andrew Jackson (3), George Washington (3), and Martha (3).

## THIRD GENERATION AND DESCENDANTS

John E. Terwilligar (3), farmer, b. Feb. 4, 1813, near Montgomery, Ohio; d.— — —1862, at Utica, Mo.; m. first, March 7, 1836 Elizabeth Jones b.— — — d.— — —. He also had three other wives. Of the second and third I know nothing except that the second lived only twelve days after their marriage and the third died about a year after marriage leaving an infant child. His fourth wife was Matilda Cosner, b.— — —; m.— — —. I think she is still living somewhere in Missouri. There were nine children in his first family but I only remember the names of N. S. (4), Frank (4), Emeline (4), Martha (4) and I think Helen (4). N. S. and Frank were soldiers in the civil war, Company I, Twelfth Regiment Illinois Volunteer Infantry. Further than this I have learned nothing of the history of his families except that there were four or five children by his fourth wife.

Catherine C. Terwilligar (3) b. Oct. 4, 1815, near Montgomery, Ohio; d. Oct. 22, 1838; m.— — —Peter Apgar, farmer, b.— — —; d.— — —; had one child, Thomas Apgar (4).

Moses K. Terwilligar (3) farmer, b. Nov. 11, 1817, near Montgomery, Ohio; d. Sept. 11, 1835. Single.

Mary A. Terwilligar (3) b. near Montgomery, Ohio, Feb. 18, 1820; d. at Montgomery, Ohio, July 11, 1905; m. first Sept.—, 1839 or 1840 Elisha Barker, farmer, b. about 1815;d. — — —; m. second, Dec.—, 1854, John W. Sage, hotel man, b. June 2, 1815; d. March 10, 1896.

Children (Barker):

James Harvey (4) and Hettie (4).

James H. Barker (4) b.— — —; d.— — —; aged about 3 years.

Hettie Barker (4) b. near Montgomery, Ohio, Oct. 16, 1846; m. Sept 9, 1873, Abram Burt Johnston, b. Feb. 7, 1849.

Children (Johnston):

Laura M. (5), Lou Fenton (5), Nellie Fayette (5), and William Burt (5).

Laura M. Johnston (5) b. Nov. 21, 1875.

Lou F. Johnston (5) b. Dec. 6, 1879; d. May 2, 1908; m. June 8, 1907, Frederick H. Hope, Presbyterian Missionary to West Africa, b. March 9, 1876.

Nellie F. Johnston (5) b. June 1, 1883.

William B. Johnston (5) b. Aug. 8, 1887.

Sarah L. Terwilligar (3) b. May 4, 1823 near Montgomery, Ohio; d. July 25, 1897; m.— — —, Eben Crist, farmer, b.— — —; d.— — —.

Children (Crist):

James (4), Nathaniel (4), Lewis (4), Mary Catherine (4) and Melvina (4).

James Crist (4) b.— — —; d.— — —; m. first — — — Clara Balser, b.— — —; d.— — —.

Children (Crist):

Florence (5) b.— — —; d.— — —. He m. second — — —Matilda —, b.— — —; d.— — —.

Children (Crist):

Frank (5) and William (5).

Frank Crist (5) b.— — —; d.— — —.

William Crist (5) b.— — —; d.— — —.

Nathaniel Crist (4) b.— — —; d.— — —.

Lewis Crist (4) b.— — —; d.— — —; m.— — — Lavina —, b.— — —; d.— — —.

Children (Crist):

James (5), Beatrice (5), Roger Eliot (5), Werner (5), Elsie (5), Katie (5) and Everett (5).

James Crist (5) b.— — —; d.— — —.

Beatrice Crist (5) b.— — —; d.— — —.

Roger E. Crist (5) b.— — —; d.— — —.

Werner Crist (5) b.— — —; d.— — —.

Elsie Crist (5) b.— — —; d.— — —.

Katie Crist (5) b.— — —; d.— — —.

Everett Crist (5) b.— — —; d.— — —.

Mary C. Crist (4) b.— — —; d.— — —; m.— — — Ovid Todd, b.— — —; d.— — —.

Children (Todd):

Chauncy Butler Todd (5) b.— —; d. — 1864, aged nine months.

May Todd (5) b.— — —; d.— — — 1873, aged seven years.

Melvina Crist (4) b.— — —; d.— — —; m.— — — — —Randall, b. — — —; d.— — —.

Children (Randall):

Two sons who died in childhood, names and dates not secured; Emma S. (5) and Katie (5).

Emma S. Randall (5) b.— — —; d.— — —.

Katie Randall (5) b.— — —; d.— — —; m.— — —, William Sarver b.— — —; d.— — —.

Eliza C.Terwilligar (3)b. June 13,1826 near Montgomery, Ohio; d. June 9, 1854; m. May 12, 1853, James Snyder Weller, b.— — —; d.— — —. Only child died aged 5 weeks.

Andrew J. Terwilligar (3) b. Sept. 8, 1828 near Montgomery, Ohio; d. July 31, 1899; m.— — —1857, Elizabeth Harper, b.— — —; d.— — —.

Children (Terwilligar):

Helen (4), Mayme (4), Albert (4), Katie (4) and Jennie (4).

Helen Terwilligar (4) b.— — —; d.— — —; m. — — — —Heller, b.— — — d.— — —.

Child (Heller):

Victor Heller (5) b.— — —; d.— — —.

Mayme Terwilligar (4) b.— — — d.— — — m. — — — — —Brown, b.— — — d.— — —.

Child: Harold Brown (5) b.— — —; d.— — —.

Albert Terwilligar (4) b. — — —; d. — — —; was married and had a daughter Verna (5).

Katie Terwilligar (4) b. Arpil 18, 1860; d. — — —; m. Oct. 18, 1899 Thomas Harris, b. — — ; d. — —.

Child: Helen Harris (5) b, — — —; d. — — —.

Jennie Terwilligar (4) b. — — —; d. — — —.

George W. Terwilligar (3) b. May 8, 1831 near Montgomery, Ohio; d. March 23, 1888; m. — — , 1856. Mary Cronover, b. — — —; d. Jan. —, 1870.

Children: Louis (4), Edgar (4), and Elida (4).

Louis Terwilligar (4) b. — — —; d. — — —, aged 21 years.

Edgar Terwilligar (4) b. — — —; d. — — —, aged 17 years.

Elida Terwilligar (4) b. — — —; d. — — —.

Martha Terwilligar (3) b. Feb. 25, 1834, near Montgomery, Ohio; d. Oct. 25, 1858; m. Oct. 31, 1855 Lloyd Smethurst, b. — — —; d. — — —; only child died in infancy.

## SECOND GENERATION

### Family of Sarah Elliott (2)

Sarah Elliott (2) b. — — 1792 near Remington, Ohio; d. Aug. 18, 1869; m. Aug. 10, 1811, John Humphrey, farmer, b. — —, 1788, near Remington, Ohio; d. Feb. 14, 1851; both buried in Miamiville Cemetery.

Children (Humphrey): Simon (3), Mary (3), William (3), Elliott (3), Samuel (3), Matthew Gardner (3), Harriet (3), and Nathaniel (3).

### Third Generation and Descendants

Simon Humphrey (3) b. June 15, 1812; d. March 13, 1819.

Mary Humphrey (3) b. Oct. 13, 1814, near Remington, Ohio; d. Feb. 17, 1895; m. — — — Jehu B. Rich, b. — — —; d. Aug. 15, 1849.

Children (Rich): Sarah (4), Mary Ann (4), Martha (4), and Harriet (4).

Sarah Rich (4) b. — — —; d. — — —. m. — — — Abraham Skinner, b. — — —; d. — — —.

Mary A. Rich (4) b. — — —; d. — — —; m. — — Lawrence Spaeth, b. — — —; d. — — —.

Martha Rich (4) b. — — —; d. — — —; m. — — — William Skinner, b. — — —; d. — — —; had three children.

Harriet Rich (4) b. — — —; d. — — —; m. — — — Riley Woodlief, b. — — —; d. — — —.

William Humphrey (3) farmer, b. Sept. 8, 1816, near Remington, Ohio; d. Oct. 2, 1894; m. — — — Rosemond Harrison, b. — — —; d. — — —.

Children: John (4), Mary (4), and Angelina (4).

John Humphrey (4) b. — — —; d. — — —.

Mary Humphrey (4) b. — — —; d. — — —.

Angelina Humphrey (4) b. — — —; d. — — —.

Elliott Humphrey (3) farmer, b. April 22, 1819, near Remington, Ohio; d. July 7, 1842; m. — — — Harriet Buckingham, b. — — —; d. — — —.

Samuel Humphrey (3), farmer, b. Oct. 14, 1821, near Remington, Ohio; d. May 26, 1891; m. — — 1844 Mary Ann Harper, b. — — —; d. Jan. 26, 1877.

Children: William (4), and Eunice (4).

William Humphrey (4) b. — — —; d. — — —.

Eunice Humphrey (4) b. — — —; d. — — —.

Matthew G. Humphrey (3), farmer, b. April 5, 1825, near Remington, Ohio; d. Oct. 30, 1910, near Kinmundy, Ill.; buried at Miamiville, Ohio; m. Aug. 21, 1851, Mary Rowan, b. Oct. 2, 1828.

Children: Harriet (4), Ennis (4), Arthur (4), Anna (4), Clara (4), Fannie (4), Margaret (4), Benjamin Franklin (4) and Elizabeth (4), all born near Montgomery, Ohio.

Harriet Humphrey (4) b. July 24, 1852; m. Nov. 25, 1872, James Cephus De Vore, b. May 20, 1851; d. Dec. 20, 1891, near Higginsport, Ohio.

Children (De Vore): Dan Lyon (5), Helen (5), Edith Olga (5), H. Clay (5), Florence (5), Seth G. (5), and Annie (5), all born near Higginsport, Ohio, except Annie who was born and died at Kinmundy, Ill.

Dan L. De Vore (5) b. Sept. 11, 1873; d. May 23, 1884, Higginsport, Ohio.

Helen De Vore (5) b. Nov. 2, 1876; m. Nov. 30, — Richard Thomas Brownrigg, b. Aug. 26, 1865, Columbus, Miss.; one son John Brownrigg (6) b. Aug. 24, 1902.

Edith O. De Vore (5) b. Dec. 27, 1878; m. June 10, 1907, John Franklin Magill, b. Sept. 20, 1875, Richmond, Mo.; one daughter, Helen Alice Magill (6) b. Oct. 20, 1908.

H. Clay De Vore (5) b. May 12, 1882; d. April 27, 1902, Canon City, Col.

Florence De Vore (5) b. May 31, 1886; m. June 10, 1906, George S. Conant, b. July —, 1887, near Kinmundy, Ill.

Children (Conant): Richard S. (6) and Walter Seth (6).

Richard S. Conant (6) b. Nov. 18, 1908, Kinmundy, Ill.

Walter Seth Conant (6) b. Sept. 10, 1909, Kinmundy, Ill.

Seth G. De Vore (5) b. Oct. 12, 1888.

Annie De Vore (5) b. June 10, 1890; d. Aug. 18, 1892, Kinmundy, Ill.

Ennis Humphrey (4), locomotive engineer, b. Sept. 28, 1854, near Montgomery, Ohio; d. — — —; m. Nov. 15, 1881, Maggie Doran, b. — — —.

Arthur Humphrey (4), farmer, b. Sept. 24, 1856; m. Dec. 24, 1884, Florede A. Eagan, b. Jan. 17, 1857; d. June 29, 1900.

Children: Jennie (5), John McClelland (5), Ruth (5), Maggie (5) and Harriet (5).

Jennie Humphrey (5) b. Aug. 31, 1885; m. Oct. 29, 1904, Ellis Wainscott, b. March 8, 1881, Kinmundy, Ill.; one child.

**John McClellan Wainscott (6) b. March 28, 1906.**

**John M. Humphrey (5) b. March 1, 1888.**

**Ruth Humphrey (5) b. Jan. 27, 1890.**

**Maggie Humphrey (5) b. June 12, 1892; d. Jan. 20, 1897.**

**Harriet Humphrey (5) b. Aug. 4, 1897.**

**Anna Humphrey (4) b. Dec. 10, 1858; m. Feb. 19, 1885, James Orval Fish, b. Sept. 12, 1848, Dupont, Ind.**

**Children (Fish): Clara Luceil (5), Harry (5), Sarah (5), Jessie Marietta (5), and John Humphrey (5).**

**Clara L. Fish (5) b. Dec. 13, 1885, Kinmundy, Ill.; m. Oct. 14, 1906, Jeduthun Henry Harpster, b. July 25. 1879 St. Peter, Ill.; one child.**

**James Fish Harpster (6) b. Jan. 31, 1908, St. Peter, Ill.**

**Harry Fish (5) b. March 1, 1888, Kinmundy, Ill.; d. Sept. 8, 1888.**

**Sarah Fish (5) b. July 31, 1896, Kinmundy, Ill.; d. Sept. 8, 1896.**

**Jessie M. Fish (5) b. Aug. 8, 1898, Kinmundy, Ill.**

**John H. Fish (5) b. March 23, 1902, Kinmundy, Ill.**

**Clara Humphrey (4) b. Feb. 5, 1861; m. Nov. 4, 1885, Homer R. Stevenson, b. April 1, 1859;**

**Children (Stevenson): Frank Milton (5) and Florence Kelly (5).**

**Frank M. Stevenson (5) b. Sept. 9, 1890.**

**Florence K. Stevenson (5) b. June 3, 1897, near Salem, Ill.**

**Fannie Humphrey (4) b. Dec. 16, 1864; m. first March 1, 1882, William Henry Simpson, b. Aug. 12, 1859; d. March 6, 1898; m. second, Sept. 19, 1907, Frank Schwartz, b. Aug. 28, 1859.**

Children (Simpson): May Belle (5) and Walter Beach (5).

May B. Simpson (5) b. Feb. 2, 1883; d. Aug. 15, 1884.

Walter B. Simpson (5) b. Sept. 6, 1885, Kingman, Kans.; m. Sept. 16, 1906, Ruby Woolley, b. April 27, 1886.

Child: Eugenia (6).

Eugenia Simpson (6) b. Sept. 7, 1907.

Margaret Humphrey (4) b. Nov. 27, 1867; m. Nov. 26, 1890, M. P. Gramley b. Aug. 5, 1861, Muncie, Ind.; have a daughter Mary A. Gramley (5) b. Feb. 5, 1896.

Benjamin F. Humphrey (4), farmer, b. Sept. 30, 1869; m. Oct. 4, 1901, Maggie Malinsky, b. April 20, 1877 Prussia; have a son William Matthew Humphrey (5) b. Oct. 26, 1908.

Elizabeth Humphrey (4) b. Feb. 14, 1872; m. Nov. 7, 1900, W. D. Gramley, b. Nov. 7, 1873, Marion County, Ill.; have a son Humphrey Gramley (5) b. April 11, 1907.

Harriet Humphrey (3) b. Sept. 27, 1827, near Remington, Ohio; d. March 17, 1888; m. — — — Jehn R. Berry, farmer and carpenter, b. — — —; d. — — —.

Children (Berry): Henrietta (4) and Matthew (4).

Henrietta Berry (4) b. — — —; d. — — —.

Matthew Berry (4) b. — — —; d. — — —.

Nathaniel Humphrey (3), farmer, b. June 1, 1830, near Montgomery, Ohio; m. March 10, 1853, Elizabeth Fitzwater, b. Oct. 27, 1833.

Children: Charles (4), Louella (4), Sarah (4), John McClellan (4) and Edwin (4).

Charles Humphrey (4) b. Jan. 17, 1854; d. Jan 21, 1881.

Louella Humphrey (4) b. Oct. 20, 1856; m. Oct. 18, 1882, Montford H. Buckingham, b.— — —.

Children (Buckingham): Mack H. (5), Ray (5), Stanley (5), Brookfield (5), Juliet S. (5) and Alfred B. (5).

Mack H. Buckingham (5) b. Oct. 7, 1883; d. April 16, 1905.

Ray Buckingham (5) b. April 25, 1885.

Stanley Buckingham (5) b. Dec. 3, 1887.

Brookfield Buckingham (5) b. June 14, 1890.

Juliet S. Buckingham (5) b. March 25, 1893.

Alfred B. Buckingham (5) b. Feb. 1, 1897.

Sarah Humphrey (4) b. Dec. 16, 1859; d. June 15, 1876.

John M. Humphrey (4) b. March 10, 1862; m. Jan. 5, 1892.

Lillie Varley, b.— — —. One daughter Elizabeth Humphrey (5) b. April, 1894.

Edwin Humphrey (4) b. July 25, 1864; m. Sept. 28, 1897, Sarah B. Oskamp, b.— — —. One daughter, Louise Oskamp Humphrey (5) b. Feb. 6, 1903.

## SECOND GENERATION

### Family of Isabel Elliott (2)

Isabel Elliott (2) b. Jan. 4, 1798, near Remington, Ohio; d. Oct. 19, 1876; m. May 11, 1815, Robert Ramsey, b Dec. 18, 1789; d. Dec. 20, 1865; both buried in North Prairie Baptist Cemetery, Bureau County, Ill.

Children (Ramsey):

Mary (3), Sarah (3), John (3), William (3), Louisa (3) and Elcy (3).

### Third Generation and Descendants

Mary Ramsey (3) b. May 8, 1816; d. aged about 2 years.

Sarah Ramsey (3) b. Dec. 30, 1819; d. April 25, 1874; m. Aug. 31, 1837, Robert Isdell, farmer, b. March 8, 1812; d. Jan. 3, 1875; both buried in North Prairie Baptist Cemetery.

Children: (Isdell):

Martha Ann (4), John Ramsey (4), William (4) Thomas Jefferson (4), George Washington (4), Robert Ramsey (4) and Sarah (4).

Martha A. Isdell (4) b. March 4., 1838; m. Jan. 7, 1857 James P. Thompson b. Oct. 18, 1835; d. Dec. 21, 1892.

Children (Thompson): William Bradford (5), Ida Francelia (5), Sarah Eliza (5), George McClellan (5), Harry Robert (5), Charles Perry (5) and Martha May (5).

William B. Thompson (5) b. Oct. 25, 1858; m. May 14, 1888, Mary Manlove, b. —— ——1860.

Ida F. Thompson (5) b. June 26, 1861; m. July 1, 1886, John J. Murray b. April 25, 1858.

Children (Murray):

Robert Thompson (6), Irene (6), Elmer James (6) and Edith Myrtle (6).

Robert T. Murray (6) b. July 27, 1887; d. Jan. 20, 1908.

Irene Murray (6) b. Dec. 27, 1889; d. Jan. 2, 1890.

Elmer J. Murray (6) b. April 11, 1892.

Edith M. Murray (6) b. Oct. 18, 1896.

Sarah E. Thompson (5) b. July 17, 1863; m. July 10, 1888, Henry P. Seip, b. Nov. 30, 1861.

Children (Seip): Walter (6), Florence (6).

Walter Seip (6) b. Aug. 3, 1890.

Florence Seip (6) b. June 30, 1895.

George M. Thompson (5) b. May 30, 1865; d. Sept. 29, 1874.

Harry R. Thompson (5) b. May 5. 1869; m. May 12, 1888, Henrietta Crompton, b. Jan. 22, 1870.

Children: Henrietta Irene (6), Mildred Florence (6) and Verna Gladys (6).

Henrietta I. Thompson (6) b. July 14, 1891.

Mildred F. Thompson (6) b. Feb. 11, 1896.

Verna G. Thompson (6) b. Nov. 12, 1901.

Charles P. Thompson (5) b. July 12, 1872; d. May 29, 1905; m. March 25, 1893, Margaret Proctor, b. Oct. 1, 1872, one daughter, Florence Thompson (6) b. Dec. 18, 1893.

Martha M. Thompson (5) b. Nov. 12, 1875; m. April 24, 1892, William H. Halling, b. May 1, 1872; one son, LeRoy Elmer Holling (6) b. Jan. 7, 1893.

John R. Isdell (4) b. Aug. 6, 1842, m. Nov. 6, 1880, to Viola Gertrude Spalsbury, b. Aug. 22, 1859.

Children (Isdell): Darius Raymond (5) b. June 19, 1881.

John Earl (5) b. May 11, 1896.

William Isdell (4) b. 1844 d. 1889.

Thomas J. Isdell (4) farmer, b. July 22, 1846; d. Jan. 8, 1908; m. Jan 4, 1870, Mary Kaar, b. June 11, 1843.

Children: Vernie Bell (5), Bertha M. (5), Alma A. (5) and Alta Laura (5), twins.

Vernie B. Idsell (5) b. Jan 4, 1874; m. Dec. 28, 1893, Elmer E. Zearing, b.— — —1872.

Children (Zearing):

Mary Alta (6) and George E. (6).

Mary A. Zearing (6) b. Dec. 7, 1897.

George E. Zearing (6) b. Nov. 4, 1900.

Bertha M. Isdell (5) b. June 30, 1875; d. July 20, 1875.

Alma A. Isdell (5) b. Nov. 10, 1880; m. Aug. 15, 1903, Herbert Bolles Coit, b.— — —1878.

Alta L. Isdell (5) b. Nov. 10, 1880; m. Feb. 8, 1908, Horace H. Burke, b. — — —1876.

George W. Isdell (4) b. Feb. 22, 1849.

Robert R. Isdell (4) b. Oct. 6, 1851; m. April 14, 1875, Fannie Studevin, b.— — —.

Sarah Louisa Isdell, b. Nov. 30, 1854, m. Nov. 23, 1878, to Andrew Maxwell, b. Feb. —, 1848.

Children: George Ninyon Maxwell, b. June 2, 1880; d. Sept. 1896.

Beula Maxwell, b. Feb. 13, 1882; m. July 9, 1904, to J. A. Wood, b. Oct. 8, 1880.

John Ramsey (3), farmer, d. Oct. 2, 1826; b.— — — m. Dec. 17, 1846, Ann Buckingham, b. Oct. 13, 1826; d. — — —, 1890.

Children: William Buckingham (4), Adelia (4), Arselia (4) Frances Ann (4) and Etta (4).

William B. Ramsey (4) b.— — —; d.— — —.

Adelia Ramsey (4) b.— — —; d. — — —.

Arselia Ramsey (4) b.— — —; d.— — —.

Frances Ann Ramsey (4) b.— — —; d.— — —.

Etta Ramsey (4) b.— — — ; d.— — —.

William Ramsey (3) b. July 3, 1826; d. aged about 4 years.

Louisa Ramsey (3) b. June 18, 1829; m. June 1, 1847, Andrew Jackson Buckingham, b. June 17, 1824; d. June 21, 1902.

Children (Buckingham): Isabella Ransey (4), Sarah Louisa (4), Alwilda (4), Kate (4) and Maud A. E. (4).

Isabella R. Buckingham (4) b. March 21, 1849.

Sarah L. Buckingham (4) b. July 3, 1851; m. May 9, 1878, William Hamilton, b. Feb. 11, 1834; d. Feb. 8, 1906.

Children (Hamilton): Robert B. (5) and William B. (5).

Robert B. Hamilton (5) b. Jan. 16, 1881; d. Aug 25,1904.

William B. Hamilton (5) b. March 26, 1888; d. Oct. 28, 1906.

Alwilda Buckingham (4) b. Dec. 10, 1852; d. Jan. 29, 1883; m. April 28, 1881, Benjamin Meyers, b. Feb. 5, 1852; d. Aug. 15, 1887; one daughter Pettie Meyers (5) died in infancy.

Kate Buckingham (4) b. July 12, 1855; m. March 31, 1887, Rev. James Maple, b. Dec. 29, 1824; d. Aug. 5, 1897.

Maud A. E. Buchingham (4) b. May 27, 1870; m. Oct. 28, 1904 John Henry Meyer b. July 28, 1869.

Elcy Ramsey (3) b. Feb. 11, 1832; m. Oct. 12, 1858, Elijah Epperson, b. Sept. 28, 1839.

Child (Epperson): Forry Isabel (4).

Forry I. Epperson (4) b. Nov. 4, 1860; m. first, George Cone, b. — — —; d. — — —; m. second, Ed. Evans, b. — — —.

Children (Cone): Geneva Elcy (5), Mary Kimbal (5), Marguerite Clarinda (5), and George Hubble (5).

Geneva E. Cone (5) b. Sept. 10, 1882; m. May 5, 1903, Charles G. Barnes, b. — — —; one daughter Florence Isabel Barnes, b. Oct. 10, 1904.

Mary K. Cone (5) b. June 5, 1886; d. Nov. 10, 1888.

Marguerite C. Cone (5) b. March — 1890.

George H. Cone (5) b. Feb. 16, 1893; d. March 1, 1893.

## SECOND GENERATION

### Family of William Elliott (2)

William Elliott (2), farmer and miller, b. Oct. 24, 1802; d. Aug. 26, 1884; m. first — — — Sarah Long,

b. Oct. 11, 1802; d. July 25, 1834; m. second — — — Sarah Hollinshead (widow) b. — — —; d. Jan. 12, 1892.

Children, 1st family: Mary (3), Simon (3), John (3), George (3), and Humphrey (3).

Children, 2nd family: Robert Ramsey (3), James Stewart (3), Simon (3), Samuel Stewart (3), Albert Douglas (3) and Sarah Matildah (3).

### Third Generation and Descendants

Mary Elliott (3) b. Nov. 5, 1827; d. — — —; m. — — — James Buckingham, b. — — —; d. — — —.

Children (Buckingham) Harriet (4), Melissa (4), John (4) and Amanda (4).

Simon Elliott (3) b. Jan. 1, 1829; d. Sept. 20, 1841.

John Elliott (3) b. April 14, 1830; d. Jan. 5, 1904; m. March — 1858, Elizabeth Martin, b. April 1, 1839.

Children: Dell (4), William (4), Arthur (4), Nettie (4) and Mary (4).

George Elliott (3) b. April 25, 1832; d. — — —.

Humphrey Elliott (3) b. Jan. 17, 1834; d. Aug. 28, 1834.

Robert R. Elliott (3) b. March 29, 1848; d. Sept. 28, 1906. He was one of several of the descendants of John Elliott (1) who made honorable military records in the civil war, and while he only served in the humble capacity of a private he found opportunity to demonstrate that he was the embodiment of every characteristic which distinguishes the good soldier. Having no personal knowledge of his army career, I have appealed to his captain, Robert Bruton, to whom I am indebted for the following; "Robert R. Elliott enlisted Feb. 8, 1864, and was honorably discharged in July 1865. After his enlistment the regiment engaged in all the Atlanta campaign which began May 1, 1864, and ended Sept. 5, 1864, and was one continuous great battle in which there was fighting night and day on some part of the line in an army of about one hundred and fifty-thousand men. After the campaign ended the regiment was ordered to Rome, Ga., and took part in the battle of Altoona Mountain and those that were not killed were with Sherman's march to the sea and through South Carolina and North Carolina and on to Washington, ending in the Grand Review there. From Washington we were ordered to Louisville, Ky., and were mustered out and discharged at Springfield, Ill., July 10, 1865. Some of the battles in which we were engaged were Lay's Ferry, Rome Cross Roads, Dallas, New Hope Church, Kenesaw Mountain, Kickajack Creek; July 22, east of Atlanta where McPherson was killed; July 28, Ezra Church, Jonesborough Station, Lovejoy Station, Altoona Mountains, took an active part in the last battle at Bentonville, N. C., and were at Derham Station when Gen. Joseph E. Johnston surrendered to Gen. Sherman." I assume that most men who were very long in the service during the civil war had frequent opportunities to show whether they were soldiers in fact as well as in name. An opportunity came to the subject of this sketch during a battle in which they were hard pressed by the enemy and their supply of ammunition nearly exhausted. Volunteers were called for, to carry a request for an additional supply. He immediately volunteered. It was necessary for him to cross an open space where he would be exposed to the hottest fire of the enemy and everyone supposed that almost certain death awaited the man who undertook it. Contrary to their expectations he reached his destination in safety. Later when asked if he had not been afraid of being killed he replied, "I never thought of it in that way; I only thought of what would become of you fellows if I didn't get through." Capt. Bruton has said "There was no braver nor more unselfish man in my regiment than R. R. Elliott" and the above seems to fully justify his estimate of the man. He was elected sheriff of Bureau County in 1902 and died shortly before his term expired. [E. F. E.] He married Dec. 25, 1872, Sarah C. Ellis, b. Aug. 16, 1853.

Children: Laura D. (4), Harry L. (4), Euretta M. (4), Jesse R. (4), George S. (4), Effie R. (4), Calvin S. (4), and Roy R. (4).

Laura D. Elliott (4) b. Sept. 16, 1873; d. Feb. 11, 1892.

Harry L. Elliott (4) b. Sept. 18, 1875; m. Jan. 14, 1902, Carrie Putcamp, b. April 13, 1882.

Euretta M. Elliott (4) b. March 27, 1878; d. June 19, 1885.

Jesse R. Elliott (4) b. March 31, 1880; m. Nov. 16, 1898, Bess Mercer, b. Feb. 24, 1883.

Children: Ethel (5), Mabel (5), Bernice (5), Robert (5), Harold (5), and Jessie Maxine (5).

Ethel Elliott (5) b. June 28, 1899.

Mabel Elliott (5) b. Feb. 7, 1901.

Bernice Elliott (5) b. Nov. 25, 1902.

Robert Elliott (5) b. April 3, 1904.

Harold Elliott (5) b. Feb. 5, 1906; d. Aug 6, 1907.

Jessie M. Elliott (5) b. March 31, 1909.

George S. Elliott (4) b. Jan. 11, 1883; d. Feb. 15, 1883.

Effie R. Elliott (4) b. Jan. 11, 1883; d. Feb. 18, 1883.

Calvin S. Elliott (4) b. Jan. 30, 1887; m. Feb. 19, 1908, Gertrude Kane, b. Aug. 15, 1884.

Child: Maurice Rollin (5).

Maurice R. Elliott (5) b. Dec. 27, 1908.

Roy R. Elliott (4) b. Dec. 18, 1893.

James S. Elliott (3) b. March 9, 1850; m. — — —.
Simon Elliott (3) b. May 3, 1852; d. — — —.
Samuel S. Elliott (3) b. Nov. 26, 1853; m. — — —.
Albert D. Elliott (3) b. Nov. 29, 1855; m. Jan. 25, 1877, Kate B. Murphy, b. March 5, 1855.

Children: William A. (4), Frank (4), Herbert (4), John (4), Mayme C. (4), Charles (4), James (4), Edward (4), and Joseph (4).

William A. Elliott (4) b. March 10, 1878; m. Sept. 20, 1904, Katherine Moran, b. — — —.

Children: Edward (5), Wilmer (5), Floyd (5), and Katherine (5).

Edward Elliott (5) b. Aug. 12, 1905.
Wilmer Elliott (5) b. Oct. 20, 1906.
Floyd Elliott (5) b. Jan. 22, 1908.
Katherine Elliott (5) b. Jan. 28, 1909.
Frank Elliott (4) b. June 2, 1881; m. May 2, 1906, Agnes Norris, b. Sept. 10, 1886.

Child: Margaret (5).

Margaret Elliott (5) b. Sept. 23, 1909.
Herbert Elliott (4) b. Feb. 7, 1883.
John Elliott (4) b. Nov. 25, 1884; m. June 10, 1908, Jennie Curren, b. July 10, 1886.

Child: Bertha Mercia (5).

Bertha M. Elliott (5) b. March 14, 1909.
Mayme C. Elliott (4) b. Jan. 25, 1886; m. Feb. 6, 1907, William J. Curren, b. Jan. 1, 1876.
Charles Elliott (4) b. Jan. 25, 1887.
James Elliott (4) b. Jan. 17, 1889.
Edward Elliott (4) b. Nov. 17, 1892.
Joseph Elliott (4) b. April 9, 1896.
Sarah M. Elliott (3) b. Sept. 2, 1858; m. — — —.

## SECOND GENERATION

### Family of John Elliott (2).

John Elliott (2) b. June 16, 1806; d. Aug. 8, 1881; m. April 26, 1836, Mary Hughes, b. Feb. 16, 1812; d. Aug. 30, 1883.

Children: Isaac Hughes (3), Jane Hughes (3), Mary Amelia (3), John Marian (3), Isabella Ramsey (3) and Charles Paddock (3).

### Third Generation and Descendants

Gen. Isaac H. Elliott (3) was born Jan. 25, 1837. Referring to his earlier life my father says: "When I came to Illinois he was about eleven years old, a bright little boy. The next summer he learned to plow corn with a single horse. Everybody plowed corn with a single horse then. He and Math. Humphrey and I worked together on his father's farm that summer. He learned rapidly at school, and when yet a small boy was considered the best speller in the school. A few brief years later he went to college at Ann Arbor, Michigan University. When he came home during vacations he didn't put on his best clothes and strut on the street, as young men sometimes do, but put on his working clothes and straw hat and came out to my place and went to work binding after a reaper, and prided himself that he was never caught on a station. He was the best man I had and always stayed until my harvest was over. He was always cheerful and had the happy faculty of infusing that same spirit of cheerfulness into others, with the result that no man sulked because he was tired or the weather was hot. When Saturday night came he saddled a colt and rode home (eight miles) and was back again before we had our breakfast Monday morning." These things might not seem worthy of mention here but the best men I have ever known were more proud of their boyhood achievements than of anything accomplished in after life; they also show that "the boy is father to the man." I have been wholly dependent on the "History of the Thirty-Third Regiment Illinois Veteran Volunteer Infantry" for the data which made it possible for me to write the military history of Gen. Elliott. This regiment had three colonels, Charles E. Hovey, Charles E. Lippincott and Isaac H. Elliott, in the order named. Both of the former being dead it fell to Col. Elliott to write the history of the regiment, which he was well qualified to do, as he is scholar as well as soldier. Col. Hovey was president of Normal University at Bloomington, Ill. when he raised the regiment, and this together with the fact that there were many learned men, not only among its officers but among the rank and file as well, led to its being called the "Normal" or "Teacher's Regiment," and sometimes in derision, the "Brain Regiment." How well Col. Elliott has written his part of the history of his regiment, under the head of "General History," how he conducted himself as a soldier and how his comrades regarded him as an officer will be shown later on by quotations from sketches, written by members of the various companies, which constitute a considerable portion of the regimental history. The things which seem to me to stand out most prominently in his character are his physical courage, his hatred of the hypocrite, his loyalty to his friends, and the entire absence of egotism. Evidencing the latter is the fact that after reading the above mentioned history I found I had to depend almost entirely on the testimony of other contributors to the work for anything personal to him. After devoting many pages to the "Field and Staff" and "Line Officers" severally, and to the soldiers in the ranks collectively, (and in some cases individually), he very generously (?) gave himself seven lines as follows: "Isaac H. Elliott, Captain of Company E, followed Potter as Major and Lieut. Colonel; was promoted Colonel in September, 1865, and was made Brigadier General by brevet to date from March 13, 1865. He was never absent from the regiment on any campaign, march or battle, except Fredericktown, and he was then a prisoner on parole. He now lives near Roswell, New Mexico." This is all he says of himself except where the mention of his name is absolutely necessary to the narrative. But his comrades were unwilling to allow him to hide behind his modesty as you will see by the following: J. H. Burham, Captain Company A, says: "Col. I. H. Elliott's admirably written historical sketch of the most important movements of the regiment will be heartily welcomed by his old comrades. No other man has ever been connected with the regiment who possessed such an intimate acquaintance with the officers and men. He knew most accurately the feelings of all classes, and possessed enthusiastic love for everything pertaining to its membership, its record and its military fame. In addition to these qualifications he has a most pleasing literary style and has the rare talent of giving descriptions of military movements in appropriate military language." His account of the Vicksburg campaign has repeatedly been referred to as being as good as anything ever written on the subject. The following over the signatures of Adjutant E. Aaron Gove and Captains Geo. E. Smith and Edward J. Lewis shows very effectually the estimate of his soldiership by those who served with him through the war: "Some of us are not willing to let Col. Elliott do all the story telling, now that the fight is over. Elliott was Captain of Company E when the regiment first assembled. A graduate of Michigan University in the class of '61, he failed to get into the three months' service with his company of college boys, and so missed Bull Run. He had all the academic qualifications for the 'brain regiment,' and others equally valuable. Nature herself had been more lavish with good gifts to him than to most of us. Tall, dark, athletic, handsome, vigorous and alert, both in body and mind, he looked to be our ideal soldier even before we knew his quality. A born leader of men, the yoke of his authority did not gall his subordinates. His enthusiasm for the cause and devotion to duty were inspiring. The drill and discipline of his company soon attracted attention, and became an example. The first blood drawn by the enemy's lead was from his company. Wounded, overwhelmed and captured in his first fight—an affair at a railroad bridge—he worked untiringly for and finally secured an exchange, against obstacles which to most men would have been insurmountable. This was his only absence from the regiment during its entire service. As early as March '62, he received a vote of confidence from the entire regiment, the only time the rank and file ever had a chance to vote. He had a just pride in the military appearance, drill, discipline and fighting efficiency of the regiment, and worked intelligently and unceasingly for its betterment. It went without saying during the service that he could get more out of them, either in drill, march or fight, than any other commander, and this after all is the supreme test. His place in the memory and hearts of his comrades of the entire regiment is secure. But what of the thirty-seven years since the war closed? Elliott was elected treasurer of Bureau County while still in the service; he ran for Congress in 1872, but was beaten, mainly, no doubt, because the thirty-third Illinois did not reside in that district; he was a Garfield elector in 1880; was Adjutant General of Illinois from 1881 to 1884, and while in that office rescued the flags of the Illinois regiments from boxes in the basement of the Capitol and had them arranged for preservation in proper cases, under a custodian, in the present flag room; he also reorganized the National Guard of the State and formed them into regiments, and compiled and published, from the scattered records, a history of the Illinois volunteers in the Black Hawk and Mexican wars. He returned to his farm, where he lived until 1894, when he went to New Mexico, and engaged in the cattle business. That he, and all his tribe, may live long and prosper, will be the sincere wish of all his former comrades in arms." In this connection I want to use one more quotation. It seems the regiment was not particularly pleased with the treatment received on the way home and at Camp Butter after arrival there. One chilly day just before their discharge they were paraded in the form of a hollow square and for more than an hour shivered in the wind while some of the notables of the State lauded the regiment and gave them advice as to their future. Commenting on this, Commissary Sargeant L. H. Prosser says: "We could see that Col. Elliott was as impatient as we were. At the first opportunity he took the colors, stepped to the front, talked to us a few minutes about our past associations; then while tears were rolling down his cheeks, he bade us good-bye, and raising the flag above his uncovered head, bade the boys give it their last cheer. Their hats went off, too, and lustily the 'Old Flag' that meant so much to them was given its last salute by the regiment as an organized body. This, their last parade, will be remembered—not for the addresses of the notable men, not for the north wind that chilled us to the marrow, but for the words and bearing of our beloved Colonel. He was a true leader of men. His presence inspired them to 'deeds of daring. His coolness in battle was their rock of safety. They admired his ability. His honesty was beyond question. He was their military hero. Other Colonels we had had—good and true men, all of them; but none of them filled the place in the affections of the men like Isaac H. Elliott. We had good reasons to believe that the Colonel fully reciprocated the affections of the men—that his chief care while in command of the regiment was their well being. Time has not lessened in any degree that loyalty of the rank and file. In their gatherings the mention of 'Elliott' brightens the eye as the tongue speaks words of loving remembrance of him." He enlisted Aug. 19, 1861 and was discharged with his regiment Dec. 7, 1865. I don't think it necessary to enumerate the battles in which he was engaged as his history is the history of his regiment and the history of the regiment is the history of the war in the part of the country where it operated. (E. F. E.)

He married Dec. 17, 1867, Elizabeth Denham, b. April 14, 1842; step-daughter of Owen Lovejoy.

Children: John Lovejoy (4), Bertha P. (4) Richard Storrs (4), Walter White (4) and, Roger Sherman (4).

John L. Elliott (4), b. Dec. 2, 1868.
Bertha P. Elliott (4), b. Aug. 22, 1871; d.— — —.
Richard S. Elliott (4) b. Feb. 24, 1873.

Walter W. Elliott (4) b. June 29, 1875; m. Louise Blodgett, b. — —.

Roger S. Elliott (4) b. Oct. 18, 1877; m. April 16, 1910, Alice Ware, b. — — —.

Children: Schuyler Blodgett (5) b.— — —.

Jane H. Elliott (3) b. March 26, 1839; m. July 3, 1861, George W. Stone, b. Oct. 22, 1830.

Children (Stone): Maude H. (4), and Cora Bess (4).

Maude H. Stone (4) b. Nov. 25, 1862; m. Jan. 22, 1901, Jeremiah Haines, b. Jan. 7, 1860.

Cora B. Stone (4) b. Sept. 6, 1864; m. Feb. 19, 1891 Edward Brooke, b. Feb. 12, 1858.

Children (Brooke): Jeannette Elliott (5) and George Edward (5).

Jeannette E. Brooke (5) b. Aug. 23, 1892; d. April 2, 1899.

George E. Brooke (5) b. Dec. 14, 1899.

Mary A. Elliott (3) b. Dec. 17, 1843; d. Aug. 28, 1896; m. Sept. 2, 1867, A. J. Washburne, b. Nov. 19, 1841; d.— — —.

Children (Washburne): Mary Christiana (4). Mary C. Washburne (4) b. May 28, 1869; m. Oct. 7, 1899, Fred Lehman, b. Sept. 25, 1866.

John M. Elliott (3) b. April 17, 1841; d. Oct. 10, 1842.

Isabella R. Elliott (3) b. Aug. 5, 1844; d. Jan. 17, 1846.

Charles P. Elliott (3) b. Sept. 23, 1849; d. July 24, 1898; m.— — —.

Nellie Whittlesey, b. Jan 25, 1855; d. Jan. 24, 1896.

ADDENDA

# ADDENDA

# ADDENDA

# ADDENDA

# ADDENDA

Ingram Content Group UK Ltd.
Milton Keynes UK
UKHW021838240323
419150UK00005B/95